DANCE IN SEQUE

SMILE

—IN HARMONY!

by PAT PRICE

Pat and Vincent Price

First published 1997
by
T. A. Whitworth,
42 Newbold Back Lane, Chesterfield,
Derbyshire, S40 4HQ.

© T. A. Whitworth

ISBN 0-9501927-6-7

British Library Cataloguing in Publication Data:

Price, Patricia

Dance in Sequence - Smile in Harmony!

I. Title II. Whitworth, T.A.

793.33

ISBN 0-9501927-6-7

Printed in Great Britain by:
LEE PRINT SERVICES
Storforth Lane, Chesterfield
S40 2TT

FOREWORD

I am very pleased indeed to publish the book of poems and cartoons by Pat Price. Although some of the material has already appeared in print it seemed worthwhile to produce a full collection in a better format.

Modern sequence dancing is a somewhat demanding form of recreation but it has its lighter side. In this volume Pat observes the foibles and quirks of the modern sequence dancer and expresses it all in verse in her own inimitable racy style; she has enlivened this further with her own original cartoons. I hope this collection of poems will bring enjoyment to many readers.

T. A. Whitworth

AUTHOR'S ACKNOWLEDGEMENTS

To *Susan Baker* and *Jon and Ray Gregson* for the typesetting and useful suggestions.

To *David Charlesworth* for the cover pages and help with graphics. David is one of Derbyshire's best-known professional artists and designers.

To *Alan Whitworth* for advice and encouragement and the preparation of the book for publication.

And last, but not least, to my dear husband Vincent who worked so hard to learn to dance just to please me.

AUTHOR'S PREFACE

It seems strange now that only a few years ago I had never heard of Sequence Dancing and that my husband had self-confessed "two left feet". He was never likely to take me to more than an occasional dance where we sat and waited patiently for the band to play a waltz or quickstep so that we could take a turn around the floor where our lack of skill would not be too noticeable among the more enthusiastic and proficient dancers. Only after retirement were we introduced to Sequence Dancing, the social phenomenon of the post-war years.

Since those days, Vincent and I have enjoyed many dancing hours both at our local dances and in various parts of the country - taking part in competitions and making many new friends on sequence dancing holidays. Our greatest pleasure, however, has been in encouraging others to join in this very pleasant activity and helping them to take their first steps on the way.

In the early days, however, we spent a good deal of time laughing at our own efforts and I began writing 'off-the-cuff' verses to amuse my dancing friends as we all shared the same trials and tribulations. With the encouragement of many friends and teachers these have now been put into a collection to be shared with all those who have experienced, or may be still experiencing, the same comic or frustrating situations - I can assure them that with a little perseverance it will all come right in the end!

My thanks go to all our teachers and the friends we have made during our dancing years, for the comic situations, the humorous remarks and snatches of conversation overheard that gave me the inspiration for the verses. I wish them all many more years of Happy Dancing.

Patricia Price

CONTENTS

RETIRING GRACEFULLY

Now at last the time has come
To put a deck-chair in the sun.
A cooling drink, a large umbrella
All made to suit a lazy fella!

But if to doze is your intention
There's just a few things I would mention
Before you settle in your chair -
And while you have some time to spare ...

Mend the door, the bolt is wobbly.
The paintwork on the sill is nobbly!
Find a screw for the sideboard drawer
There's a mouldy patch on the bathroom floor!

Dig the garden, sow some seeds,
Mow the lawn and kill the weeds.
There's something nasty in the shed
And greenfly in the flower bed.

Scrub the yard and sweep the drive,
Make sure the goldfish stay alive,
And just before you do the shopping
Remember that the car needs washing.

Let's go cruising down the Nile!
Climb a pyramid with style!
Or hire a 'plane and fly to France!
OH! BLOW IT ALL!. . . . . . .

LET'S LEARN TO DANCE!!

THE SWINGING SIXTIES

After years of office typing
    Came the day I must depart.
I said, "Goodbye" to all my friends
    With quite a heavy heart.
The desk I loved looked lonely!
    My chair looked very sad!
And suddenly I remembered
    All the good times I had had.

I told myself, I'd have more time
    To spend upon myself.
But then I found that too much time
    Had left me "on the shelf ".
What could I do to fill my days?
    I'm active, bright, and merry!
I'm growing old, but glowing too,
    And mellow, just like sherry!

But then one day, it came to me!
    I knew just what I'd choose!
I'd join the Sequence Dancers
    And learn those Swings and Blues!
It did not seem so very hard
    And the music's very nice.
I'd go along, and join the Club
    And try it once or twice.

The first big step I had to take
    Was just to climb the stairs!
They were so steep and twisting,
    They caught me unawares!
My breath came short, in painful puffs.
    I really felt quite dizzy!
But now I'm up, I'll be all right,
    Although I'm in a tizzy!

I try to find an empty seat,
    But almost every chair,
Is covered by a handbag,
    So I know I can't sit **there**!
It is a golden rule, you see,
    When articles are spied ...
This signal means, "Please keep off!
    This space is occupied!"

Our leader then took up the floor
    To show us what to do.
With patience and with fortitude
    For I hadn't got a clue!!
Then moving in amongst us
    He called out, "Running Spin!"
He wouldn't pick on me so much
    If he knew the spin I'm in!!

He has a paper called 'a script'.
    It's all he seems to need.
It's something like my knitting script
    But mine is easier to read!
I wonder what is "b.o.f."!
    It does seem rather rude!
My partner says, "It's ball of foot!"
    I must have misconstrued!

Our leader says, "It all begins
    Left foot diag the wall".
The experts then all smile and nod,
    They seem to know it all.
They dance away, and then we hear
    A very rueful, "Coo ...
What's gone wrong? What have I done?
    I'm still diag the loo!"

3

The 'gramophone' plays long and loud
       To keep us on the move.
And everything is swinging
       Until it skips a groove!
And then it all grinds to a halt,
       We're all confused and scattered!
We've turned to stone, bewildered, lost!
       Our confidence is shattered!

But now I am a dancer!
       I've learned the Bambi Blues!
I'm going out tomorrow
       To buy some dancing shoes!
I'm trotting out those tricky words,
       Like telemark and corté ...
Hip Twist! Fan! and Rumba Walk!
       Which make me feel quite naughty!

And so you see, when 60 comes,
       It isn't just "the end".
It's only the beginning
       For playing "Let's Pretend".
The years have rolled away again.
       We're 'seductive', 'young' and 'slim'
And for our age, and for our shape,
       Just what good shape we're in!!

4

WESTON-SUPER-MARE

Oh! What a lovely time we have
    when we go to Weston.
We jump on the coach, all merry and bright,
    All with our Sunday best on.

We sing a gay song, as we roll along,
    And munch on our crisps, and our buns.
And so we arrive, all ready to jive ...
    But we've all got a pain in our tums!

We feel such a thrill, as we enter the room
    To dance on that wonderful floor.
The man who sells shoes, with the buckles and bows
    Is usually, just by the door.

The shoes stand in rows, just to tempt us fair maids.
    With 'diamonds' all sparkling, and gleaming!
We "ooh" and we "aah", and we're tempted, of course!
    And "bang" goes all the 'housekeeping'!

We love to see Ted, as he walks on the floor,
    Together with the elegant Sue.
They sway, and they glide, to the music of Bryan ...
    So we think we'll have a go too!

But its not quite the same, 'tho we give it our best!
    We're all a bit jumpy and jerky!
Instead of the grace and the glide of a swan,
    We look like an old barnyard turkey!

Going home on the coach, we're all happy and tired.
    We've had such a wonderful day.
The sea breeze, and music, have lifted us up,
    And the cobwebs have all blown away.

So, here's to the days out at Weston.
    May they go on, for ever and ever.
And one day, we'll dance like Sue, and like Ted
    Then, **won't** we be jolly clever?!

TEA DANCING

Just before noon, we set out with glee
For a dance at our club, and a nice cup of tea.
Dressed in our best, and skirts with a twirl ...
Our noses are powdered, each eyelash in curl.

The men are all handsome, the ladies are 'dolly',
The music is playing, and it's ever so jolly!
Our knees may be creaky, but we press on with a grin.
It's mind over matter, and the dancing will win!

With cha-cha and rumba, just look at the style!
We're Fred, and we're Ginger, just for a while.
But I've kicked Mrs. B - my regret is profound ...
But I know she'll get me, next time around!

Mrs. B's very cross, 'cos I'm dancing with Rita
Who's her bosom pal when we dance the Veleta.
She'll be even crosser, when she finds out that Perce
Has told me my rondés are better than hers!

We're all so intent on improving our skill
And we'll all get it right, I know that we will.
We all do our best to dance it with style,
But as Teacher says, "It just takes a while."

We're standing up tall, and lifting our nose.
Trying to remember all the heels and the toes.
Sometimes we wonder, "Will it ever come right!"
We'll concentrate hard, and then it just might!

Teacher reminds us about shoulders that slump!
Too much projection, back there in the rump!
When we're dancing the Samba, look out for our volta
And just eat your heart out, young John Travolta!

We're all in good shape, there's no doubt at all.
And when we are dancing, we're having a ball!
With troubles behind us, we're happy and gay,
All keeping fit, the Tea Dancing Way.

*'But I've kicked Mrs B -
my regret is profound
But I know that she'll get
me next time around!!'*

THE NEWCOMER

When first we venture to embark upon these tribal dances
  It's hard to walk in through the door, and meet enquiring glances.
We always take the vacant seat that's nearest to the door
  And concentrate intently, on the pattern on the floor!

A smiling face will then approach, we are so jolly grateful!
  Things look good, we're thawing out, and feeling not so hateful.
It seems that every kindly soul has knowledge to impart
  And as we're led upon the floor, at least we've made a start!

Balmoral Blues? Is that a fling? Apparently, it's not!
  We lock step here, and lock step there, and zig-zag quite a lot.
And just as we begin to do this very tricky thing ...
  Oh! Blow it all! The music's stopped! Now, what's a Sindy Swing?

Step and tap, and then again, and then we turn right round.
  My partner is a little fierce, and swings me off the ground!
Dance a square, and then do this! Oh Lord! Whatever next!
  And now they shout "Serida!" No wonder I'm perplexed!

We rumba and we tango, and who's this Sally Ann?
  When I started, I was 'lady', but I've finished dancing 'man'.
I love my honeysuckle, it's growing round my porch
  But here they try to tell me, it's another kind of waltz!

We're rather short of 'fellers', so I have to dance as man!
  I partner Wynne, and Gladys, and Emily and Gran!
But when we dance a rumba, although they're very game ...
  Because it's so romantic, it's never quite the same

My Saga must be sagging, I really haven't got it.
  I know it's got an 'oozit', which then becomes a 'wotsit'.
It goes on to a 'thingy' and ends up with a 'twiddle'
  But I'm blowed if I remember the bit that's in the middle!

I'm trying hard to learn it all, it's become a big ambition.
  For now you see, it seems to me, I have a special mission.
And when the lady by the door, stares only at her shoes ...
  I'll say with pride, "Come on, my dear, let's do Balmoral Blues".

I'll be so proud, as we whirl round, she'll think my dancing's thrilling!
  She'll never guess my knees are weak,
                and that my corns are 'killing'.
I'm sure she'll think I really am, a very clever "cookie".
  I'll not let on, and she won't know, that I am just a "rookie".

'The lady at the door stares only at her shoes.'

THE TAXI QUICKSTEP

When I was young - a handsome lad
    The dancing scene just made me sad.
The ballroom floor was not for me ...
    I'd two left feet, as all could see!

I had to sit and watch the girls,
    With twirling skirts, and bobbing curls,
And envy all those lucky lads
    Showing off their latest fads.

And then at last, I learned the skill!
    I set about with iron will
To waltz and quickstep, tango, rumba
    And make myself a 'classy number'.

In taxi quicksteps I'll surpass
    And dazzle every lovely lass!
With roguish eye, I'll laugh with glee
    To see those 'cuties' queue for me!

But somehow, things have all gone wrong!
    Why did it take so very long?
I don't remember growing old
    Or notice how the years had rolled!

When taxi quickstep time is here ...
    I tremble, and I quake with fear!
Please God! Let me survive once more
    This marathon around the floor.

I take the lady, first in line,
>Whose girth is so much more than mine!
My nose is pressed against her bust!
>And what is more, my toes are crushed!

A little lady, small and neat.
>I'll dance this one right off her feet!
I do! But as I double spin and twist ...
>I find she's dangling from my wrist!

At last, here's one just heaven sent.
>The size is right. But Oh! That scent!
Her footwork's neat, spin turns in order
>But now I smell of Estée Lauder!

I'm sixty plus, so the name I'll change
>For the taxi dance is too much strain
My breath's too short - I've missed my chance
>My 'ticker' protests - "Not that taxing dance!"

So when the 'Taxing' dance comes round
>I'll steal away and run to ground.
Until I hear a waltz or blues
>Then I'll return with strength renewed.

And if they should say I'm passed my prime
>When I creep out at Taxi Time
I'll smile and say, "I've not been far -
>Just ouside to check my car!"

SATURDAY NIGHT

Oh dear! What can the matter be?
  The pensioners' rave-up is here on Saturday!
The neighbourhood's stunned, and shocked by it all
  As the Senior Citizens arrive for their ball.

They're all quite mad, and barmy of course ...
  And over-excited by the thought of a waltz!
There's going to be trouble - of that there's no doubt!
  So the Neighbourhood Watch gets ready to shout!

Here come the lager-louts, fingers will point!
  That lady is smoking, it must be a joint!
With bags full of hash, and plenty of 'pot'
  They really are wicked, this Old Tyme lot!

Mr. Policeman, can you come quick!
  They're dancing a Saunter! It's all a bit thick!
It's gone 10.30 and the music's still thumping
  At this time of night, they should turn into pumpkins!

As they tango and cha-cha, with arms all a-wave
  It's easy to see that they're really depraved!
They're dancing the rumba!! We know what that means!
  It's a love dance you know, and really obscene!

This tribal dancing is really too much!
  With Veleta, and blues, and foxtrot, and such.
They're all too old for this mating game
  And they're giving the place a really bad name!

And they expect to continue 'till 11 p.m.
  Supposing we let them? Exactly, what then?
For after the dancing, when they've all had a 'jar'
  I've seen a woman get in a man's car!

At 11 p.m. they should all be in bed.
    Their teeth in a glass, when prayers have been said.
We cannot allow these older young folk.
    To kick up their heels, and enjoy a good joke!

Put them away, keep them well out of sight!
    If they all get too happy, they'll quarrel and fight!
We can't hear our telly, their music's too loud
    We must kick them out, this troublesome crowd!

They mustn't be happy, or get over-zealous
    They're ever so bad ... Oh no! I'm not jealous!
It seems that their sins are too bad to mention ...
    So down with all those receiving a pension!

'The Senior Citizens arrive for their ball.'

THE RAFFLE

Today, we are having a raffle.
    We all have our tickets of pink.
We all get rather excited,
    As it's drawn while we're having our drink.

We are all asked to bring in our trinkets
    Just to add to the choice of the 'loot'.
So we empty our drawers, and our attics
    To find what we can that will suit.

There's a very nice cup, with its saucer.
    I've seen it being unpacked.
Though the saucer is chipped, the cup's very nice
    And only a little bit cracked!

I was recently, really quite lucky
    With a copy of "Measure for Measure".
And this I may say, just made my day.
    It's really a prize I shall treasure!

But lest you should think I'm a highbrow,
    Let me just say, that I'm not!
My table is old with a wobbly leg
    And the book's the right size for a prop.

There's a vase that looks very pretty,
    Which was brought in by Maudie, last week.
I won it with glee, and carried it home.
    And then I found out that it leaked!

Now I've a ring on my table,
    And the polish has gone very black.
I've returned it today, and hope very much
    That Maudie will just win it back!

There's a picture of sand, with some donkeys.
And a hat that says, "Kiss Me Quick".
A sandwich of cheese, with some chutney!
I must say I think that's a bit thick!

There's a record of Dame Nellie Melba
That's seen a few better days.
A guide book that's ever so helpful
If you're lost in Hampton Court maze!

There's a kit bag, with tin hat and gas mask.
And also a bicycle pump.
A pig in a poke, and a camel
That seems to be minus a hump!

The raffle is drawn! And Lord Bless Me!!
My knees have gone very weak.
They've called 43, and I've won it ...
Again it's that ****** vase, with a leak!!

'Today we are having a raffle.'

CRÊPE CALYPSO

Percy bought himself some shoes
    Just to chase away the blues!
Soles of crêpe, and tops of leather,
    Just the thing for mucky weather!

Percy wore them up and down,
    In the country, in the town.
So proud was he of his new shoes ...
    Every day, these shoes he'd choose!

On the day of the big tea dance,
    He gave his other shoes no glance!
"I'll wear my crêpes, I love them so!"
    And off for dancing he did go.

But at the dance, Perce looked a clown!
    As all the folks began to frown!
Squeak, Squeak! they heard, all round the floor
    Was it mice? Or just a door?

Oil can in hand, they rushed around,
    But still they heard that squeaking sound!
"What can it be?" the dancers cried
    As every door was oiled, and tried.

The quickstep music seemed to flow ...
    But there again - squeak squeak slow!
And as the tango reached its peak ...
    There it was, slow slow squeak!

And Perce was there, quite unperturbed.
    He whirled around without a word.
Did he know? Or did he care?
    His shoes were causing all the stir!

The band played loud to drown the sound,
    And still Perce danced, and squeaked around!
The dancers were all close to tears,
    With splitting heads, and aching ears.

So please, Dear Perce, we do implore!
    When you're on the dancing floor,
To join in quicksteps, and the blues ...
    For Pity's Sake! Get dancing shoes!

'Squeak, Squeak! They heard all round the floor!'

'Oil can in hand they rushed around.'

RALPH'S ROVING EYE

Ralph Ducane, a handsome 'cad'
    Lost his eye when just a lad.
But naught cared he, as time went by,
    So proud was he, of his glass eye!

He polished it both day and night.
    And held it up to catch the light!
Never was an eye so 'jammy'
    Shone to perfection with a 'chammy'.

With sparkling orb tucked into place
    And rakish smile upon his face ...
Off to the tea dance, looking cute
    Immaculate in pale grey suit.

The dance in swing, he swung and swayed,
    With a twist and twirl, as the music played.
When all at once, he heard a "plop"
    He really thought his heart would stop!

The eye bounced once, and then took flight!
    And rolled away, first left, then right!
Ralph's roving eye was uncontrolled
    As round the dancers' feet it rolled!

On hands and knees, Ralph crawled around,
    But the roving eye could not be found!
The dancers thought, "A new dance for sure!"
    And **all** crawled round upon the floor!

But then a lady caught his eye ...
    She grabbed it, just as it flashed by!
She held it up, admired its glitter!
    And buffed it on her dancing slipper!

"Dear lady, you have caught my glance! ...
   May I ask you for a dance?
To tell the truth, for a week or two
   I've had at least, one eye on you!"

The lady smiled, "Well, thanks a lot!"
   But Ralph had caught her on the hop!
She hung her coat up on a peg ...
   And then retrieved her wooden leg!!

*'Off to the tea dance looking cute,
Immaculate in pale grey suit'*

'On hands and knees Ralph crawled around'

19

THE DANCING YEARS

Tango here, and rumba there,
With two basic, then a square.
Remember now, what I've been told ...
Get into a closer hold!

Shoulders back, chin held high.
Tango steps are thigh to thigh!
Keep on going, keep it neat!
And never, never, wag my seat!

Heel then toe, and toe toe heel.
Sometimes, what a fool I feel!
Slow quick quick, and quick quick slow.
Or is it, slow slow quick quick, slow and slow?!

Chassé, corté, twinkle, hover.
Wing and weave, it's all no bother!
Watch my open telemark ...
See my spin turn! What a lark!

My hair is grey, but what's it matter?
Dancing stops me getting fatter!
When I'm on the dancing floor ...
Who would guess I'm 64?!

LAST WALTZ

Jessie called round here today,
To say that Doll had passed away!
I am so sad, it makes me weep
For Doll was at the dance last week!

Doll was big, and rather tall
And no good on the floor at all!
We tried to dodge her when we could
For Doll, it seemed, was made of wood!

Poor Doll! She loved her dancing so,
But stepped on each and every toe.
She scattered dancers everywhere
As she whirled round without a care.

Last week, it all came to a head!
But I regret the things I said!
The last dance played, and what a sin!
I saw that Doll was waltzing Jim!

"Look here, Doll. That's not right!
You know that Jim brought **me** tonight!
And when it's nearly closing time
You know the last waltz should be **mine**!"

How could I know I'd feel such pain?
Poor Doll would never dance again!
I should have said, "Enjoy the dance ...
And make the most of every chance!"

Now Dolly's gone! We miss her fun!
She was so **nice** to everyone!
No wonder I'm so very sad ...
Doll's dance with Jim was all she had!

So Doll is off, her steps to try
At that big ballroom in the sky!
What will happen? Heaven knows!
I pity poor St. Peter's toes!

THE NEW FANGLED TANGO!

It just takes two to tango
That's what they always say,
But when we try to tango
Our feet get in the way!
So it's never very clear to me
To which two they are referring
Although we do our very best
A depressing thought's recurring...
If when we dance the tango
They say it just takes two
They simply weren't referring
To the likes of me and you!

23

OVERTURE

If you are over sixty
And still feeling bright and frisky,
I'm sure, like me, you love those Sequence Dances.
The music's very pretty
And I hum each little ditty
Whilst ignoring all those disapproving glances!

I'm learning how to rumba!
Soon I'll be a classy number!
Pushing forward always on my toes.
My hip twist may be tragic,
But my Alemana's magic!
As I try my best to match the Latin pose!

I'm pushing out my hips
As I pivot, and I slip,
And then I try to swing it just like Elvis!
But I heard a sort of crack!
And I think I've 'ricked' my back!
And there's a funny sort of pain there in the pelvis!

I'm sure I look a chump
When I'm waggling my rump,
As many other learners have before me.
But I swing it and I sway,
I don't care what others say,
As long as others don't simply just ignore me!

My breath is getting shorter!
My knees are full of water!
Sometimes the pain will really make me shout!
But I'm smiling to the end
Although it's 'just pretend'
As I need a stick to help me walking out!

Sometimes, I like to show
Just how much I really know!
I help the rest to really get it right!
They should know I'm being helpful
When I say their footwork's dreadful!
So why is their grateful smile a little tight?

I offered just today
To show someone the way,
And helped correct a tricky little feature.
She said, "Please wear your glasses
When you come into my classes
And then perhaps you'll recognise *your teacher*!!"

YOU KNOW YOU'RE GROWING OLD
WHEN YOU NOT ONLY REMEMBER
THE WORDS OF A SONG, YOU CAN
ALSO UNDERSTAND THEM!

PAS DE DEUX

My husband and I ... are learning to dance!
        We're both keen as mustard, of course!
But we never agree, and it's easy to see
        It's going to end in divorce!

We bicker, and quarrel, whenever we dance,
        Whether it's one steps, or two steps!
We just can't agree who's getting it right
        When we're doing the old steps or new steps.

I say, "It's a samba!" He says, "It's a rumba!"
        So we both get a little bit tense.
Our steps are not matching, the direction's all wrong!
        He says it's all **me**, and I'm dense..!

I count, one two and three! He counts, two three
                    and four!
        And even, seven, eight nine and ten!
So we do a quick skip, and a couple of hops!
        Then start to argue again!

He treads on my toe, and ladders my tights!
        Once more, my big toe is bare!
He says, "Sorry! But really you know
        That your foot should not have been **there!**"

He holds me too tight and I simply can't breathe
He hugs me as tight as a bear
I begin to feel dizzy, my head's spinning round
And I have to retire to my chair.

He says I'm too heavy, I should learn to relax
But I'm sure I'm quite light on my feet
So I just tell him so but the next thing I see
Is my partner's returned to **his** seat.

He gets it all wrong when we're doing a waltz,
He says, his lead I don't follow!
I answer, "What lead?! ... and just so you'll know ...
I'm not coming dancing tomorrow!"

So, I'll not go again! I'm giving it up!
Dancing and marriage don't mix!
What's that he says? It's time for the dance?
"Yes, love! I'll be there in two ticks!!"

He whirls me around, and I'm dancing on air!
But soon I'm counting to ten!
For the flush on my cheek, isn't purely romance!
It's the pain in my big toe, again!!

POSTMAN'S KNOCK

When the postman calls to leave my scripts
  Sent by Brockbank-Lane,
Excitement mounts as I digest
  These new dances, once again.
A brand new waltz, a new gavotte
  I persevere to learn.
With brain confused, but iron will
  I note each twist and turn.
But before I've really got it
  And quite sure just what I'm at ...
The postman calls again too soon
  And drops more upon the mat!
Again I study night and day
  To keep up with the score.
But once again, before 'ere long
  The postman brings me more!!
And still I keep on dancing
  But my brain is rent asunder!
And I find the new gavotte
  Is mixed up with the rumba!
I really try to get it right,
  No other could be keener!
But halfway through 'Miranda'
  I find I've danced 'Marina'!
I dance the waltz so proudly
  With style, and lifted chin.
But teacher says, "I said 'Westmount'
  And you are dancing 'Westlynn'!"
I tango the 'Manhatten'
  But it really isn't fair,
When all the others get it wrong
  And dance the 'Debonair'!
I'm really good at cha-cha-cha!
  but when I am the leader,
To show just how the 'Chino' goes

It turns into 'Corrida'.
So pity my poor postman
    With large, and laden sack!
And also poor souls like me
    Who haven't got the knack!
Instead of posting three or more
    Through my worn front door.
Can I **please** have only **one**.
    I really don't want more!
And then, maybe, I'll stand a chance
    Of keeping 'in the swim'
With only one a month to learn
    I think that I could win!
Otherwise, I'll have to wait,
    And dance just what I can.
And that will be Balmoral Blues,
    Sindy Swing, and Sally Ann!

'The postman calls again too soon
And drops more upon the mat!'

THE SURVIVORS

At our tea dance, recently,
  It just occurred to me!
These are the SURVIVORS
  Who dance, and drink their tea!

For we were there before the days
  Of plastic, and the pill!
Those who caught us scrumping
  Were 'coppers' ... not 'The Bill'.

'Made in Japan' meant rubbish!
  'Gay' meant light in manner!
And everything in 'Woolies'
  Only cost a tanner!

'Time-sharing' meant togetherness!
  And not a home abroad!
'Hardware' was a local shop!
  And 'Software'? ... no such word!

We married first, then set up house.
  The other way was shady!
A husband was important
  Before you had a baby!

Sixpence in your pocket
  Would take you to the 'pics'
With a little bit left over
  To buy some fish and chips!

We doted on our film stars!
  Robert Taylor, and Clark Gable.
And girls wore curls upon their head
  To look like Betty Grable!

The lads wore 'short back and sides'
  All slicked down with Nufix!
And parted it like Cary Grant
  Just like on the 'flicks'.

We'd never heard of yoghurt!
  We had liver oil and malt!
But our baked spuds were better
  With the taste of ash, and salt!

The potato men with glowing carts,
  Were such a welcome sight.
We gathered round, and warmed our hands
  On cold and foggy nights.

Then there was "Amami Night"!
  And Californian Poppy,
Banana Split, Plush Nuggets,
  Snowcreme, and treacle toffee.

The trams came rattling down the street
  With traffic on each side.
So it really was quite tricky
  When getting on to ride.

Some people went inside the car,
  And some of them, upstairs.
Upstairs, was called "outside the car"
  Because no roof was there!

Then one day in September,
  We heard machine guns rattle.
We saw the Spitfires overhead
  As the precious "few" did battle.

We heard the 'bulls' and sirens,
  And the crashing of a land-mine.
So we went down to the shelter
  And lit another Woodbine!

1/10d worth of meat!
  Our rations were so thin!
But, somehow, we all managed
  With the help of Vera Lynn!

4oz of marg, 2oz of tea,
    And very little soap.
But of some things, there was plenty!
    We had comradeship! And hope!

So, here's to the SURVIVORS
    Who knew about romancing!
Long may they live to drink their tea
    And continue, "Happy Dancing".

They may be a bit old fashioned,
    With many little quirks.
But they did their deals with handshakes!
    And somehow, IT ALL WORKED!

The lads wore 'short back and sides'
All slicked down with NuFix!

SONGS OF THE DANCING BIRDS

The pretty little sequence birds
    Are gathering in their flock.
Upon their village hall they swoop,
    To dance till 4 o'clock.
They call their roosting place 'The Dance'
    And to meet there is essential,
For without their weekly gathering,
    They turn all temperamental.

Each has it's own particular perch,
    No other must encroach.
"This woolly mat reserves that perch!"
    The clucking sounds reproach!
And when a stranger ventures
    His dancing skills to test,
The local birds all twitter,
    "There's a cuckoo in the nest!"

The sequence birds have plaintive cries -
    "The floor is much too sticky!"
"Too slow", they cry, and then, "Too fast".
    "This dance is much too tricky ...
Rumba spirals left and right -
    I really feel quite groggy!"
"The coffee's weak!" "The tea's too strong!"
    "My ginger nut's all soggy!"

The mating habits of these birds
Seem to follow one set pattern.
Each cock bird dancing with his mate,
Is most inclined to happen.
Except in a 'progressive'
When the cock birds have their fling,
And they're allowed to change their mate
And spread their little wings.

Then there is a special breed,
Who have their special cry ...
"Hot Off The Press!" they warble,
"Do come and have a try."
"It's H.O.P.", they flutter,
"This dance is really great!
Let me show you how it goes,
And keep us up to date!"

These birds are called the 'Hoppers'
And they earn our admiration.
They often travel far and wide
With the utmost dedication.
But sometimes little dancing birds
Begin to feel quite bilious
When the Hopper's dedication
Becomes too supercilious!

But Modern Sequence Dancing Birds
Are a breed quite set apart,
And deep within each dancing breast
There lies a generous heart.
Just remember, if you're tempted -
Their little boat to rock,
You won't upset just one small bird ...
You're taking on the flock!

TEA DANSANT

The doors open at two
And I'm first in the queue!
For I'm keen on my special seat!
I'm in at a sprint
Although my arm's in a splint!
Rose nearly beat me last week!

Rose's gold locks
Are kept in a box!
Although she says they're her own!
If I grab her wig
She won't look so big
So she can just leave my seat well alone!

Bill dances with me
And fetches my tea.
But Bill can be really suggestive!
It's nudge, nudge, and wink!
So I go a bit pink
When I nibble my chocolate digestive!

Bert's a bit rummy!
He really is funny!
Sometimes his words get confused.
When we dance bota fogos
He says, "Ah! fota bogos!"
Then wonders why we are amused!

We are dancing a corté.
Bert calls it a sauté!
And mixes his dancing with cooking!
He calls the Samara
The "Saunter Cascara!"
So we titter when Bert is not looking!

Glady's friend
Seems on the mend!
After her tangle with Gwen!
But the poor little chap...
The cause of the scrap,
Has never been heard of again!

There's a nice little man
Who comes when he can.
"But don't tell the missus!", says he.
He comes for a rest
But dances with zest,
And dunks ginger nuts in his tea!

There's a new chap today
But I'm sorry to say
He's rather a 'smarmy-type' person!
There's a problem as well
That 'his best friend won't tell!'
Let's hope that the problem won't worsen!

*If I grab her wig
She won't look so big.*

DANCE! AND GROW YOUNG!

I REFUSE TO GROW OLD GRACEFULLY!
    I'm fighting all the way!
I still feel bright and eager
    To 'cut a rug' and 'make the hay'!

But then again, I must confess,
    It doesn't seem quite fair,
When I feel like 'the morning after'
    Although I've not been anywhere!

Sometimes, I feel quite desperate!
    I think, "Whatever next!"
When I'm looking for my glasses
    So I can find my specs!

But when I dance the rumba,
    I impress the dancing locals.
My eyes shine bright, but they don't know
    It's just sunlight on bifocals!

Sometimes, my legs get weary,
    And buckle at the knees!
If I could buckle my new belt
    I'd be so awfully pleased!

Today, I felt quite angry,
    And stamped around a bit!
I found my bra was back to front
    But seemed a better fit!!

But still, I mustn't grumble
    About the pains that lurk!
Some bits are really painless ...
    But those few bits don't work!

But as a sequence dancer
    I just ignore it all!
When I dance with Mrs. Millington
    I'm the belle of 'Friendship Hall'.

Mrs. M's a bit forgetful!
    Although she is a leader.
She often sings, "Old Folks at Home"
    While we're dancing the **Serida**!

But I'm putting on my make-up,
    And keeping up a front.
I'm pulling on my dance shoes
    Whilst trying not to grunt!

The music starts, and all is well.
    I quarter turn, and chassé.
The clock turns back, and once again
    I'm only just a **lassie**!

So I'm growing old protesting!
    The rocking chair can wait!
No one knows, and none shall guess
    I'm past my 'sell-by' date!!

BASIL

Basil Billings was the best
    Of teachers in the land!
He'd made himself an expert
    Exactly as he'd planned!

To Spain he went, to learn to do
    Flamencos, bright and zippy.
And then to Honolulu,
    To learn the Hula, smooth and hippy.

He travelled into Russia
    To study Cossack dances.
And then again, to Burma
    For those exotic stances.

But then, one day, he was dismayed!
    A fellow teacher chaffed!
"You really think you know it all,
    But that's not so!" he laughed.

"You've been across to India,
    To Zanzibar, and France!
How come, with all your travels
    You can't do the BUCHA dance?

"The BUCHA dance?" said Basil.
    "How could I have missed it?
Please show it to me right away!"
    He pleaded; then **insisted**!

His tormentor then just winked his eye.
     "I'm afraid I can't," he sighed.
"You have to learn it at first hand,
     Taught by the Mooli tribe!"

"The Moolis live in the Amazon.
     In the forest they all dwell.
You'll have to go and seek them out.
     And take them gifts, as well!"

So, Basil set off right away.
     So woeful, and so humble
To think that he had missed the dance
     They all did in the jungle.

He journeyed through the forest.
     And how the bugs did bite!
He sweltered in the daytime,
     And chilled all through the night.

But at last! He found the Moolis!
     His joy was unsurpassed!
He settled down and waited
     Until a long, long time had passed.

And then, one day, the Mooli tribe
     Gathered for their hop!
And Basil's great excitement
     Nearly caused his heart to stop!

They wore their feathered headgear.
A bone adorned their nose!
Complete with all their war paint
But very little clothes!

The drums began their throbbing beat!
The Moolis formed a choir!
They came out from the darkness
To gather round the fire.

Then all at once ... the tribe rose up!
They gave a fearsome shout!
A mighty cry of BUCHA ...

RY TARMIN
BUCHA RY TARMOWT
BUCHA RY TARMIN
ANSHAYKIT ORLABOWT!!!!

They wore their feathered headgear.
A bone adorned their nose!

43

DON'T YOU BELIEVE IT!

I say ...
"Don't you believe it!"
When they say ...
"He doesn't bite!"
Or, when they say ...
"We've just popped in!"
Because you **know** they'll stay all night!

We have heard ...
"I promise, if elected ..."
It doesn't mean a thing!
And ...
"The tank is full of petrol!"
Or ...
"Sometime, give me a ring!"

"It's going to be a sunny day!"
But it rains! ... and you've no umbrella!
You trust your best friend with your life!
Then find she's nicked your fella!

"Things can't get worse!"
It's often said.
But then, of course, **they do**!
The 'quick drink' that is promised
Will last an hour or two!

So, I say ...
"Don't you believe it!"
Though they promise not to laugh
When they persuade you into jiving!
And cramp grabs you in the calf!!

HAS ANYONE SEEN GRANDMA?

If you are looking for Grandma
    You won't find her there
For Grandma has deserted
    The old rocking chair.
You won't find her in...
    You haven't a chance!
For Grandma's gone off
    To her Saturday Dance.

If it's a sitter you're after
    I'm afraid it won't do
For Grandma is out
    And so is Aunt Lou,
They're dancing tonight
    Down at the Hall
Better wait a few days -
    Then give her a call.

And if Grandma's not there
    When you contact her number
It's because she's in town
    Where she's learning the rumba.
And when she won't answer
    And the 'phone's off the hook...
Her type writer's clicking
    'Cos Gran's writing a book!

45

EDNA

Edna is 90 - It's so hard to believe...
She's still so neat and serene!
We sang 'Happy Birthday' and toasted her health
With tea, and strawberries and cream.

I know Edna sighs as she sits in her chair
For once she was best of them all
But her feet keep on tapping - and I'm sure she's aware
That she's still the Belle of our Ball.

For we know that Edna's not there in her chair
That's only the outside you see.
And Edna in spirit is out on the floor -
Still youthful, still lively and free.

Edna's blithe spirit will never grow old
And her heart is as light as a feather
With wings on her heels she dances with us
As gay and as graceful as ever.

So to all those like Edna who now sit and watch
Don't think we don't know or don't care
We know you've been young and remember it well...
And our pleasure's increased when you're there.

STAY AS SWEET AS YOU ARE

Among the dark and fearful days
We knew in time of War
I met a lad - my G.I. Joe
A Stranger on our Shore.

A handsome lad with dark brown eyes...
And he became my chum.
He gave me nylon stockings
Chocolate bars and gum.

A lonely boy so far from home
He taught me how to jive.
He showed me how to rock and roll
And dancing came alive!

Then came the day when Joe moved on
The parting brought such pain.
One last goodbye, a sad farewell...
We never met again.

But if I should meet my G.I. Joe
Will he be tall and raunchy?
Or will he be overweight,
Bald and fat and paunchy?

One thing's for sure I hope he'll say
If side by side we sit...
"Gee Honey, throughout the years
You haven't changed a bit!

THE THINGAMAJIG

When I won the raffle
At our dance, recently,
I stepped up with my ticket
As pleased as I could be!

But when the prize was yielded
Into my eager hands,
My winning smile just vanished!
It wasn't what I'd planned!

The little vase of roses
Was merely for display!
My prize was something different,
And I took it with dismay!

I smiled, a little weakly!
And said, "Thanks, so very much!"
But what **was** this curious object,
So unfriendly to the touch?

It was hard, and sort of lumpy!
With a handle on the side.
A kind of greeny-purple,
With a mouldy growth inside!

I could tell it didn't like me!
 So avoiding any fuss,
I simply made my mind up
 To leave it on the bus.

I left the bus so gaily,
 And walked off, down the street.
Then suddenly, my blood ran cold
 When I heard some running feet!

"Excuse me!" said a young Cub Scout.
 "Today is Bob-a-Job!
You left this 'thingy' on the bus!"
 So I had to pay a bob!!

I took it home, still wondering
 What on earth this thing could be.
I placed it on the sideboard
 Where it sat, and frowned at me!

My neighbour from just down the road
 Called on me one day.
And when she saw the 'wotsit'
 She blanched! And turned quite grey!

She tried just to ignore it!

But it had magnetic powers!

So to try and make it pretty

I popped in a bunch of flowers!

But the flowers soon were shrivelled!

I watched their petals drop!

"That's not a vase!" my neighbour cried,

"It's just an old door-stop!"

So as the door was banging,

I wedged it with my 'foe'

But as I turned to walk away,

I tripped! And broke my toe!

Then I gave it to the 'Jumble'

With a happy little sigh.

It really is amazing

What some weird folk will buy!

When Aunty Clara came to tea,

With a gift all tied with string.

In my head I felt a thumping,

And my ears began to ring!

It was the awful 'thingamajig'
   And as I turned an ashen hue,
I heard my Aunty saying,
   "I'm sure this is JUST YOU!"

I know you will have guessed it!
   It's as plain as it can be!
Although Aunty likes my sister,
   SHE'S ALWAYS HATED ME!!

"I'm sure this is just you!!"

IT DOES SEEM SUCH A PITY

It does seem such a pity,
      But we find it everywhere.
When we have our dances
      There are no gentlemen to spare!

The ladies come in twos and threes,
      And sometimes, just as one.
But when it comes to pairing up
      Where have their partners gone?

So the ladies dance together,
      And although they're very game,
A romantic waltz or rumba
      Can never seem the same.

And then there is a point or two
      When close hold is a must,
How can they get together
      When there's the problem of the bust!

I have to find a partner
      From the ladies left in line,
Who is just a little taller
      And whose front will fit with mine.

If hers will settle on the top
      Then the problem is all gone.
But it's a very different matter
      When mine, meets hers - head on!

Men don't dance together.
    For them there is no need.
In any case, they never would
    Agree, just who should lead.

Men are told that they're in charge,
    All through their dancing years.
So the question of, "Just who leads who?"
    Would always end in tears!

So come on, all you missing men!
    Get out of that armchair!
We're not looking for Gene Kelly
    Or the skill of Fred Astaire.

We only need a gentle man!
    Then how our eyes would glisten!
The dance-shy male would soon find out
    Exactly what he's missing!

BALLY DANCING!

What's the name of that little dance?
You know, the one we used to do!
It had a little twiddly bit,
And then a turn or two.

You must remember that little dance!
It went sort of slow, with quick steps.
It had that funny three point turn,
And then some lockwards backsteps.

Oh! What's the name of that little dance?
It was my favourite thing!
I think it had a oozit ...
And then a wrong side wing.

You know! We danced it all the time!
And you always partnered me!
It had a two, and three, and four,
And then a one, two, three!

I'm sure it's not a tango,

And I don't think it was a rumba.

It might have been a cha-cha-cha ...

What was it's name I wonder?

Tomorrow, I'll ask our teacher,

And request another chance

To dance again the 'wotsitsname' -

My very favourite dance!

"What's the name of that little dance?"

TWO LEFT FEET

For many years I've managed
    Without a special ruse,
To tell my right foot from my left
    When putting on my shoes.

So, why is it, on the dance floor,
    Of sense I seem bereft,
And find it such a problem
    To tell my right foot from my left?

I've tried so many cunning ways
    To conceal my little failing.
I've marked my right foot with a cross
    So all should be plain sailing.

But when the order's left foot first,
    Here comes another riddle!
Did I mark my right or left?
    And again I have to fiddle.

I do a little hop and skip,
    And although my fudging's deft,
The teacher calls across the room ....
    "NOW TRY THE OTHER LEFT!"

You wouldn't think he'd notice
    A little hop or two,
But he has a very beady eye
    As teachers often do.

I have a very useful chart
    Which shows feet black and white:
I wonder if I wore odd shoes
    It might help to get it right.

It would be, oh! so simple
    If we had just one foot each,
And make it really easy
    For those who had to teach.

But when the lesson's over
    And I fall into my bed,
With natural turns and telemarks
    Still spinning in my head ...

I am so very grateful,
    For those who strive like me -
The Good Lord gave us just two feet,
    SUPPOSE HE'D MADE US THREE!!

THE BLACKPOOL BELLE

How I loved to ride
          on an old Blackpool tram!
And jump off at the Tower for a dance.
With the boy that I loved,
          who loved waltzing with me,
To me, this was truly romance.

The Lancashire lassies
          on leave from the mills,
In cotton dresses, all fluttering and gay,
Linked arms as they strolled
          the length of the Prom,
And sang all the songs of the day.

The ballroom was magic,
          with it's sound and it's lights;
Reginald Dixon the man we adored.
As the Wurlitzer rose
          from somewhere below
The music thundered and soared.

'Tho you may go to Spain,
          or Greece or Corfu,
You won't know how grand it could be,
For a girl of the thirties
          who longed all the year
For just one week, at Blackpool-on-Sea.

The years have gone by-
                more than a few!
But I still return for a day,
To the joys of my youth
                and recapture the spell,
While the breeze blows the cobwebs away.

For today is soon gone,
                'tho we don't see it go -
And yesterday's here all too soon.
But the music plays on
                in the great Blackpool Tower,
And the magic is still there in that room.

And we all ride the tramcar
                to the end of the line,
'Tho one by one, friends alight on the way,
For pressing appointments
                of their own they must keep,
As they come to the end of their day.

But some will remain,
                as we journey along,
Brightening our way with their smile.
And we all travel on,
                on the big tramcar ride,
To the end of our own Golden Mile.

So I still love to ride
                on the old Blackpool tram,
And jump off at the Tower for a dance.
And the boy that I loved -
                still waltzes with me,
For we've shared a lifetime's romance.

GOING SOLO

I never look in the mirror and say -
    "My word! Today I look old!"
But then you see, I don't see very well,
    At least that's what I've been told.
When I was a girl my hair was quite dark,
    And just seemed to fall into place.
Now I arrange the locks I have left,
    As the rest has fallen from grace.

I don't want to be a grey lady
    In crimplene and cardies and such.
I want dance shoes that sparkle and glitter,
    'Tho my bunions don't like it too much.
I spurn the white shoes with large matching bag,
    Bursting apart at the seam,
My handbag is small and all it contains
    Is a lipstick, powder and cream.

I refuse to be stored on a dusty old shelf
    Just because I'm around sixty plus.
And I don't like the driver who says, "OK Gran!"
When I show him my pass on the bus.
I'm longing to say, "Young man, come with me ...
    Come dancing and kick up your heels.!"
And after we've danced a few cha-cha-chas
    We'll see just how sprightly **he** feels.

I play a few records and dance all alone,
    Just to make sure my joints are not freezing.
Sometimes it seems the record's gone wrong,
    But it's only the sound of me wheezing.
There are times when I'm feeling downhearted
    And I don't seem at all the old me,
But I soon buck up with the first aid of food,
    And a large transfusion of tea.

When the music begins, dancing is fun,
    But soon I'm again reminiscing
Of the days in the past when a strong pair of arms
    Steered me round dance floor and kitchen.
But those days are gone, and may never return.
    Ah well! And alas! - that's as may be!
So I settle today for a tango or two
    In the arms of a nice gentle lady.

So I'll add a few sequins to my little black dress,
    And I'll rough up the soles of my shoes,
Then the clock will turn back as I show off my skill
    In the foxtrots, tangos and blues.
And my family are pleased when they come to call
    And they find me not sitting alone.
They 'phone me to say, "We came round today -
    But it seems YOU'RE NEVER AT HOME!"

RONDE DE JAMBE

I really couldn't do without
  My text book just for dancers.
I read each page so carefully,
  So now I know the answers.

I find the words so handy
  When I am in a spot.
I'm never stuck for words you see,
  I just trot out the lot!

Recently, my neighbour
  Complained about my cat!
I said "b.o.f! c.b.m.p.!"
  She couldn't answer that!

I thought the wisdom of my words
  Was just an inspiration!
But she performed a natural turn,
  And then a hesitation!

She did a little two-step,
  With a lockstep in the middle.
I did a sort of zig zag,
  And then an outside swivel.

I swayed to left, and then to right,
  And then I did a weave.
She didn't like my hockey stick,
  So she began to leave.

And just when I thought, maybe -
   I was going to win,
A rather forceful zephyr
   Caught me on the shin.

Then she turned to walk away,
   And with a kind of leer ...
I showed her my best ronde de jambe
   Directly to her rear!

She did a splendid natural spin!
   And before my pride diminished,
I went into a quick reverse
   Complete with running finish!

I said "b.o.f ! c.b.m.p !"

THE BEGINNERS' QUADRILLE
(with apologies to Lewis Carroll)

"Will you walk a little faster?"
      said a teacher to a snail,
"There's a couple just behind us
      and they're treading on my tail.
See how eagerly the experts
      and medallists advance!
They're waiting on the side lines -
      will you come and join the dance?"

"Will you, won't you, will you, won't you,
      will you join the dance?
Will you, won't you, will you, won't you,
      will you join the dance?"

"You can really have no notion
      how delightful it will be,
When you've really got the pattern
      and can trip around with glee."
But the snail replied, "Too hard, too hard!"
      and gave a look askance,
Said he thanked the teacher kindly
      but he would not join the dance.

Would not, could not, would not, could not,
      would not join the dance.
Would not, could not, would not, could not,
      would not join the dance.

"What matters it how long it takes?"
   his teacher friend replied.
"There is another snail, you know,
   across the other side.
You'll find it all so easy
   if you give yourself a chance.
So turn not pale, beloved snail
   but come and join the dance."

"Will you, won't you, will you, won't you,
   will you join the dance?
Will you, won't you, will you, won't you,
   will you join the dance?"

But as the teacher walked away,
   the humble snail espied,
The charming little lonely snail
   across the other side.
He forgot about his shyness,
   and thought only of romance -
"Come take my hand my pretty dear
   and show me how to dance."

"Would you, could you, would you, could you
   show me how to dance?
Would you, could you, would you, could you
   show me how to dance?"

PLAY IT AGAIN SAM!

When I was young, and in my prime,
  In tune with latest fads,
I danced the moonlight nights away
  And charmed the local lads.

Slim as a reed, with tossing curls,
  In love with each film actor,
I'd twist and twirl around the floor,
  Lips coloured by Max Factor.

I danced the jive with G.I. Joe,
  A regular 'killer-diller'
At Hammersmith Palais with Joe Loss,
  And best of all - Glen Miller.

Then somehow, all the years flew by,
  And although I thought it wouldn't,
My figure kept on filling out,
  Especially where it shouldn't!

I didn't seem to find the time
  To dance the light fantastic.
Some bits of me had worn right out
  And been replaced with plastic!

But now I'm over sixty,
  And fancying my chances;
For I have joined my local club,
  Where they do those sequence dances.

Balmoral Blues, and Rumba One,
    And then a waltz or foxtrot.
I even try a jive or two,
    And fancy I'm a hot-shot.

It seems that through the passing years
    When I was getting stout,
There was still a dancing dolly
    Just waiting to get out.

No longer young, but **still** in my prime,
    In tune with latest fads,
I dance the afternoons away
    And charm the local 'lads'!

And when sometimes it's pointed out,
    I'm too old for this addiction,
I smile, and say, "Old age, you know,
    Is **achievement**, not affliction!"

So play it again, Sam! Just for me.
    Life's rhythm never changes.
Just the outside wears away
    As nature re-arranges.

Bifocals steam up, joints will crack,
    I'm puffing like a tractor!
But the smile I smile, is good as new -
    Still coloured by Max Factor!

ROCK AROUND THE CLOCK

2 o'clock, it's Sindy Swing,
    And I'm full of verve and vigour,
Locking here and locking there
    In spite of ample figure.
Full of swing and lots of sway,
    With twinkling toes and heels.
The rhythm has me in it's spell,
    And oh! how good it feels.

By 2.15 I'm in my stride,
    But the tango's quite a hurdle,
My partner holds me much too close,
    We almost share one girdle.
She likes to make it snappy,
    And there's no other couple like us,
But all that snap plays havoc
    With a neck with spondylitis.

At half past 2 we're waltzing,
    And Fred's asked me for a dance.
He's quite a fancy dancer,
    And I'm grateful for the chance.
But he whirls me round with gusto
    Until my ligaments feel torn;
And I know at any moment
    He's going to stamp upon my corn!

At 3 o'clock we all collapse,
    Quite weary from the battle,
And we are all so very grateful
    To hear those tea cups rattle.
But soon when we've been watered,
    And slipped out for 'these and thoses'
We're back upon the dance floor
    With freshly powdered noses.

At half past 3 we rumba,
     And I think I'm on 'Come Dancing'.
I'm sinuous and sexy,
     But I know my luck I'm chancing,
For as I dance my hip twist,
     With the accent on the hip,
With fingers crossed I breathe a prayer
     In case a disc should slip.

4 o'clock and it's all been done,
     Well - just until next week.
We're out of breath and sore of foot,
     With fragile knees that creak.
But there's no-one like tea dancers,
     I'm sure you will admit,
To show the world just what it means
     To have stamina and grit!

'We almost share one girdle!'

FOR THE RECORD

"We're tired of those old records!"
The dancers were not happy!
"Please give us now a proper band,
With musicians bright and snappy."

Their leader gave a weary sigh,
"I'll see what I can do.
On Saturday, we'll have a band
With musicians just for you."

On Saturday, the band arrived,
Billed as "The Dancing Hot-Shots"
In raggy jeans they seemed more like
A band of local despots!

To music loud and thumping,
As the Hot-Shot Boys gyrated,
The fillings in our teeth came loose,
And our ears were perforated.

We rocked and rolled, and shook and shaked,
Then feeling quite emotive -
We plunged into a Twist or two
And tried the Locomotive.

But when the clock struck 12 o'clock
Then came the devastation -
As dancers rummaged in their bags
For pills and embrocation.

Then once again, they took a chance,
And booked "A Latin Trio"
But young they weren't! And what is more -
They'd never been near Rio!

In dusty suits, and shaggy locks -
Their music old and tired!
The dancers shuffled round the floor
Depressed, and uninspired.

"We must be more up tempo",
The frustrated dancers sighed,
"We'll try Welsh Morgan's organ ...
'The Rhondda Valley's Pride'."

So Welsh Morgan brought his organ,
And at first this seemed good news!
But just when things were swinging ...
He went and blew a fuse!

"Enough's enough!" the dancers wailed,
"We're sorry we've been wayward.
Please give us back our Bryan Smith,
Jimmy Locke, and Dennis Hayward!"

HOUSEWIFE'S CHOICE

My mind is in a turmoil
A poem's just begun ...
But just look at all that washing!
There's so much to be done.

I've thought about my subject
And decided what to do
But what to have for lunch today
I haven't got a clue!

I don't want to go to Betta Buys
To shop for bread and meat,
Or find that special offer
For Sunday's tea time treat.

And then of course there's dancing...
We are learning that new dance!
Which means I've got to concentrate
Or else I have no chance.

But I want to write my poetry
And finish my new book.
I haven't time to dust the room
Or make the beds and cook.

I'll just dash off another verse
And then I'll mop the floor.
On second thoughts I really must
Just write a few lines more.

For now I've got the rhythm
I can't just leave it there
When will I ever clean the house?
Quite frankly - I don't care!

FINALÉ

And now at last, I've finished!
  At least, just for a while.
No more fish and chips for tea,
  It's Cordon Bleu, with style!

I'm going to polish windows,
  And take my dog out for a walk!
I'll feed the cat, and iron a shirt,
  And clean each knife and fork!

The cupboards will be tidied,
  Before they burst asunder!
But while I dust and polish
  I can still rehearse the rumba!

And just in case you wonder
  Why, at the time I keep on glancing,
I've got to hurry through the chores
  So I can go out dancing!

But soon, I know, the fun will start!
  My head will soon be buzzin'
And from my old typewriter
  Rhymes will spill out by the dozen!

So, if you want another book,
  Just post through my front door,
A simple card, with simple words ...
  Dear Pat ... One more Encore!

THAT'S ALL FOLKS!

Finally, I cannot do better than to quote Mr. John Gould, Fellow and Examiner, UKAPTD.

"Always remember that dancing should be enjoyed, so try to make each and every session a happy one, not only for yourself, but for everyone present."

KEEP DANCING, STAY HAPPY, AND TRAVEL SAFELY.

Patricia Price